Good for Me
Play and Exercise

Sharon Coan

Publishing Credits

Rachelle Cracchiolo, M.S.Ed., *Publisher*
Conni Medina, M.A.Ed., *Managing Editor*
Jamey Acosta, *Content Director*
Dona Herweck Rice, *Series Developer*
Robin Erickson, *Multimedia Designer*

Image Credits: Cover, pp.1, 8 ©iStock.com/Robert Churchill; p.3 ©iStock.com/ImagesBazaar; pp.5-6, 11-12 ©iStock.com/Chris Futcher; p.7 Jose Luis Pelaez Inc./Getty Images; p.9 ©iStock.com/Peter Mukherjee; Back cover ©iStock.com/GlobalStock; all other images from Shutterstock.

Library of Congress Cataloging-in-Publication Data

Coan, Sharon, author.
  Good for me : play and exercise / Sharon Coan.
    pages cm
  Summary: "Get moving! Get thinking! Exercise your body and brain. This book will give you ideas for things to do."— Provided by publisher.
  Audience: K to grade 3.
  ISBN 978-1-4938-2152-5 (pbk.)
1. Exercise—Juvenile literature.
2. Physical fitness—Juvenile literature.
3. Health—Juvenile literature. I. Title. II. Title: Play and exercise.
  RA777.C64 2016
  613.7ʹ1—dc23
                                                                    2015014973

Teacher Created Materials

5301 Oceanus Drive
Huntington Beach, CA 92649-1030
http://www.tcmpub.com

ISBN 978-1-4938-2152-5

© 2016 Teacher Created Materials, Inc.

What can I do?

I can do this.

I can do this.

I can do this.

I can do this.

I can do this.

I can do this.

I can do this.

I can do this.

Words to Know

exercise

play